U.S. GOVERNMENT AGENCIES

WHAT DOES THE DOJ DO?

★★★ DANIELLE HAYNES

Published in 2026 by The Rosen Publishing Group, Inc.
2544 Clinton Street, Buffalo, NY 14224

Copyright © 2026 by The Rosen Publishing Group, Inc.

All rights reserved. No part of this book may be reproduced in any form without permission in writing from the publisher, except by a reviewer.

First Edition

Editor: Danielle Haynes
Book Design: Rachel Rising

Photo Credits: Cover, ftwitty/iStock; Cover, pp. 1, 3–24 Madan Designer/Shutterstock.com; Cover, pp. 1, 3–24 Art Posting/Shutterstock.com; Cover, pp. 5, 7, 9, 11, 17, 21 Mehaniq/Shutterstock.com; p. 4 dizain/Shutterstock.com; p. 5 Tada Images/Shutterstock.com; p. 6 https://commons.wikimedia.org/wiki/File:Foundation_of_the_American_Government_by_Henry_Hintermeister.jpg; p. 7 https://commons.wikimedia.org/wiki/File:EdRand.jpg; p. 8 Meir Chaimowitz/Shutterstock.com; p. 9 https://commons.wikimedia.org/wiki/File:Pam_Bondi_in_2025.jpg; p. 10 SORASIT SRIKHAM-ON/Shutterstock.com; p. 11 mariakray/Shutterstock.com; p. 12 Lana U/Shutterstock.com; p. 13 Chase Clausen/Shutterstock.com; p. 14 RUBEN M RAMOS/Shutterstock.com; p. 15 Dzelat/Shutterstock.com; p. 17 Gorodenkoff/Shutterstock.com; p. 18 nyker/Shutterstock.com; p. 19 https://commons.wikimedia.org/wiki/File:President_Nixon_meeting_with_Attorney-General_Eliott_Richardson_and_FBI_Director-designate_Clarence_M._Kelly_-_NARA_-_194514.tif?page=1; p. 20 Drazen Zigic/Shutterstock.com; p. 21 Suwatchai Wongaong/Shutterstock.com.

Cataloging-in-Publication Data

Names: Haynes, Danielle.
Title: What does the DOJ do? / Danielle Haynes.
Description: Buffalo, New York : PowerKids Press, 2026. | Series: U.S. government agencies | Includes glossary and index.
Identifiers: ISBN 9781499453058 (pbk.) | ISBN 9781499453065 (library bound) | ISBN 9781499453072 (ebook)
Subjects: LCSH: United States. Department of Justice–Juvenile literature. | Justice, Administration of–United States–Juvenile literature.
Classification: LCC KF5107.H38 2026 | DDC 347.73–dc23

Manufactured in the United States of America

Some of the images in this book illustrate individuals who are models. The depictions do not imply actual situations or events.

CPSIA Compliance Information: Batch #CSPK26. For Further Information contact Rosen Publishing at 1-800-237-9932.

CONTENTS

WHAT IS THE DOJ? 4

BIRTH OF THE DOJ 6

THE CABINET 8

U.S. ATTORNEYS' OFFICES 10

FEDERAL OR STATE? 12

TIMELINE OF A CASE 16

THE WATERGATE SCANDAL 18

A CAREER WITH THE DOJ 20

GLOSSARY 22

FOR MORE INFORMATION 23

INDEX 24

WHAT IS THE DOJ?

What do police officers, prosecutors, and prison guards have in common? They're all part of the justice system. The justice system handles crimes, from **investigations** to imprisoning someone found guilty.

The U.S. Department of Justice (DOJ) has a special role within the United States's justice system. The DOJ prosecutes federal-level crimes. Some crimes break state laws while others break federal laws. Some break both! When someone breaks a federal law, it's the DOJ's job to investigate and prosecute the crime. Most lesser crimes break only state laws. Sometimes the state and DOJ work on cases together.

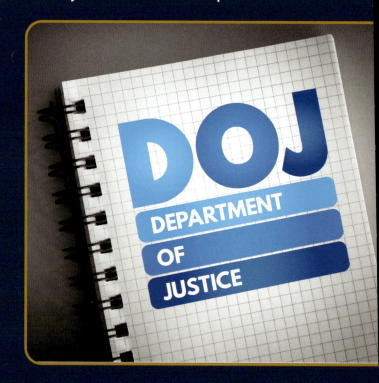

AGENCY INSIGHTS

Prosecutors are lawyers who represent the government in both state and federal trials.

The Department of Justice's headquarters is in the U.S. capital, Washington, D.C.

BIRTH OF THE DOJ

The U.S. justice system has existed for as long as the United States has been a country. Shortly after the founding of the country, President George Washington named Edmund Randolph Jennings as the first attorney general. The attorney general is the top **law enforcement officer** of the federal government.

In 1870, the U.S. Congress created the DOJ to keep the country safe and protect civil rights. The attorney general oversees the DOJ. Over the years, the government has created more than 40 agencies within the DOJ. These organizations handle specific kinds of crimes or duties.

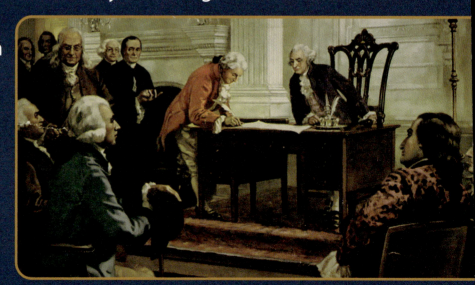

AGENCY INSIGHTS

Civil rights are laws that make sure people receive equal opportunities regardless of the color of their skin, religion, gender, and other characteristics.

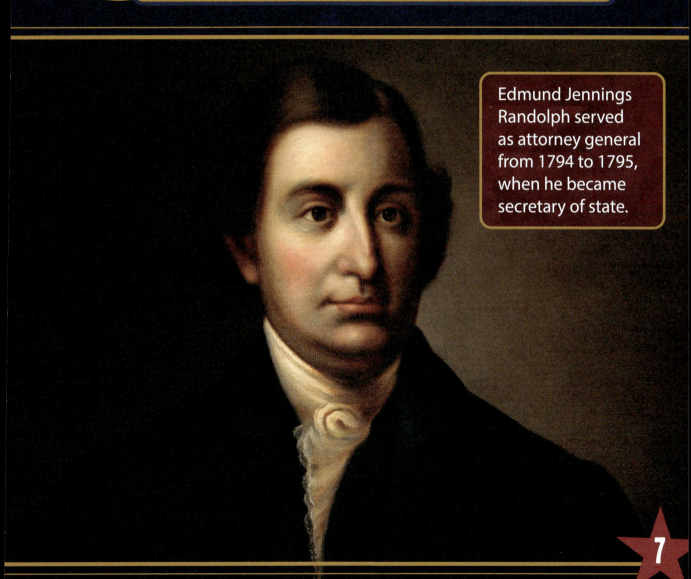

Edmund Jennings Randolph served as attorney general from 1794 to 1795, when he became secretary of state.

7

THE CABINET

The DOJ is one of 15 cabinet-level departments. These departments operate under the executive branch of the government. The U.S. president is the head of the executive branch and appoints each of the people who lead the 15 departments. The U.S. Senate must then approve those leaders, including the attorney general.

The heads of the departments—most of whom are called secretaries—are some of the president's most important **advisors**. Some people think the president shouldn't be allowed to pick the attorney general. That's because the DOJ might have to investigate the president. This is called a conflict of interest since the attorney general might be divided between their loyalty to the president and following the law.

AGENCY INSIGHTS

The 15 cabinet departments are: agriculture, commerce, defense, education, energy, health and human services, homeland security, housing and urban development, interior, justice, labor, state, transportation, treasury, and veterans affairs.

In early 2025, President Donald Trump named Pam Bondi (right) as his attorney general.

U.S. ATTORNEYS' OFFICES

The DOJ is a vast organization with thousands of employees and handles roughly 400,000 cases in a year. To make this more manageable, the department has attorneys all over the country in different districts. There are 94 federal districts, each with a U.S. attorney to oversee operations. Each state has at least one district, though bigger states such as California and New York have up to four.

The U.S. attorneys' offices prosecute federal crimes that happen within their districts. Each district relies on many people, including prosecutors or lawyers, **paralegals**, and other workers. There are also courthouses and judges in each district.

AGENCY INSIGHTS

Federal judges aren't part of the DOJ or the executive branch, but instead the judicial branch. They are appointed by the president and approved by the Senate.

If a federal case goes to trial, the U.S. attorney's office must present **evidence** to a judge in a courthouse such as this one.

FEDERAL OR STATE?

The Founding Fathers established the United States as a federal republic. That means power is shared between the government of the individual states and the whole country. All people in the country must follow U.S. laws no matter what state they live in.

But each state also has its own set of laws. Some are the same as the federal government, and some are different. State laws tend to be more specific, dealing with things such as divorce and child **custody**. The DOJ investigates only broader, federal crimes, such as civil rights and **immigration** issues.

Crimes committed at national parks are often considered federal because they happen on federal land.

Sometimes, federal and state laws **overlap** and local police and the Federal Bureau of Investigation (FBI) work together. For example, kidnapping is generally handled by only local or state police. However, if a criminal kidnaps someone and takes them from one state to another, it also becomes a federal crime.

In some cases, a crime may be prosecuted in both state and federal courts. There may be differences in punishment too. In the worst cases—murder—a state's highest punishment might be life in prison. The federal government, however, could sentence the same person to the death penalty.

The FBI is the top law enforcement agency in the United States and investigates crimes just like local police officers do.

TIMELINE OF A CASE

Because there are so many kinds of crimes and agencies within the DOJ, each case can look a little different. Most follow a general timeline, though:

- INVESTIGATION: DOJ investigators gather evidence and find out who did the crime.

- CHARGES: Prosecutors file charges against the person they think did the crime, called a defendant.

- **PLEA** BARGAIN: The defendant may admit they did the crime in an agreement with prosecutors.

- TRIAL: If the defendant pleads not guilty, the case goes to trial. The defendant is either found guilty or not guilty.

- SENTENCING: If guilty, a judge or jury decides on a punishment for the defendant.

- APPEALS: The defendant can ask for a new case called an appeal.

AGENCY INSIGHTS

Before prosecutors can charge a defendant, a group of **civilians** called a grand jury must review the evidence and agree. The grand jury then issues an indictment, which lists the charges.

When a case is presented to a grand jury, it's a little like a trial.

THE WATERGATE SCANDAL

One of the most well-known DOJ cases is the Watergate **scandal**. Watergate is the name of an office building in Washington, D.C. In 1972, burglars broke into the Watergate offices of President Richard Nixon's Democratic challenger in the presidential election.

Attorney General Elliot Richardson appointed a special prosecutor—Archibald Cox—to investigate the burglary to find out if Nixon knew about or planned it. After the FBI found evidence that Nixon tried to cover up the break-in, the president stepped down in 1974. Dozens of other government officials were found guilty in the case, including former Attorney General John Mitchell.

THE WATERGATE COMPLEX

Attorney General Richardson (left) named Archibald Cox to lead the case to avoid conflicts of interest. Nixon (center) appointed Richardson as attorney general, so Richardson might have had reason to protect the president in the investigation.

A CAREER WITH THE DOJ

If a job in the DOJ sounds like it might interest you, keep in mind there are many different career paths. A prosecutor would need to study law in college, while those who want to be an FBI agent would need special training.

The DOJ offers many programs and scholarship opportunities for young people interested in working for the agency. There are many internship programs, which are work experiences for college students who then get school credit. Even younger students can learn more about careers in the FBI with the organization's teen and youth academies. It's never too early to start learning about a possible career in the DOJ.

AGENCY INSIGHTS

More than 115,000 people work for the Department of Justice across the globe.

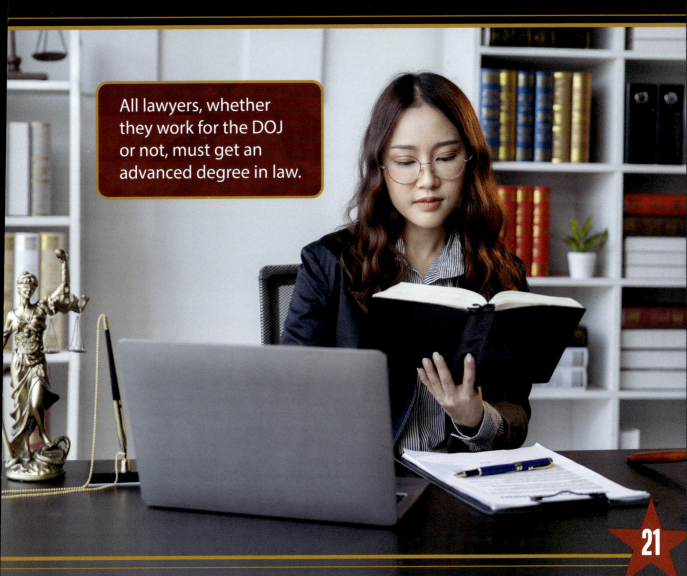

All lawyers, whether they work for the DOJ or not, must get an advanced degree in law.

21

GLOSSARY

advisor: Someone who gives advice or helps others make decisions.

civilian: A person who's not a member of law enforcement or the military.

custody: To be in charge of or take care of another person such as a child.

evidence: Something that shows that something else is true.

immigration: The act of coming to a country to settle there.

investigation: The process of examining and gathering evidence about a crime.

law enforcement officer: A person who works for a government department that is formed with the purpose of making sure laws are followed.

overlap: To have something in common with.

paralegal: A person who works as an assistant to a lawyer.

plea: A defendant's answer to a charge or indictment.

scandal: An occurrence in which people are shocked and upset because of behavior they find morally or legally wrong.

FOR MORE INFORMATION

BOOKS

Hamilton, John. *FBI*. Minneapolis, MN: Abdo & Daughters, 2022.

Koon-Magnin, Sarah, and Ryan J. Williams. *The US Criminal Justice System: A Reference Handbook*. New York, NY: Bloomsbury Academic, 2024.

Rebman, Nick. *Watergate*. Mendota Heights, MN: Focus Readers, 2024.

WEBSITES

Attorneys General of the United States
www.justice.gov/ag/historical-bios
Learn more about every person who's served as attorney general in U.S. history.

Federal Bureau of Investigation
www.fbi.gov
Visit the official website of the FBI.

Publisher's note to educators and parents: Our editors have carefully reviewed these websites to ensure that they are suitable for students. Many websites change frequently, however, and we cannot guarantee that a site's future contents will continue to meet our high standards of quality and educational value. Be advised that students should be closely supervised whenever they access the internet.

INDEX

A
attorney general, 6, 7, 8, 9, 18, 19

B
Bondi, Pam, 9

C
cabinet departments, 8, 9
conflict of interest, 8, 19
Congress, 6

E
executive branch, 8, 11

F
Federal Bureau of Investigation (FBI), 14, 15, 18, 20

G
grand jury, 17

J
Jennings, Edmund Randolph, 6
judges, 10, 11, 16
judicial branch, 11

N
Nixon, Richard, 18, 19

P
police, 4, 14, 15
prosecutors, 4, 5, 10, 16, 17, 18, 20

R
Richardson, Elliot, 18, 19

S
state laws, 4, 12, 14

T
Trump, Donald, 9

W
Washington, George, 6